Birds in a Durham Village. A photographic and written record of birds in the Great and Little Lumley and the surrounding around the areas 2020 to 2021.

Written by Robert Bishop

In the early days of my retirement, I saw a Grey Heron looking for a mid morning snack in the middle of the Cong Burn. It stood for several minutes in the same location only occasionally moving its position as its eyes were firmly on the water. I took several pictures and it opened a door to the natural world. On many local walks I observed the natural world in and around the Lumley area. During walks around the Lumley area and on its borders in places like Rainton Meadows I have observed many different bird species. Some of the birds reside in the area all year round while others migrate depending on the season. It is a confusing picture as some birds of the same species are resident while others are migratory. I have seen ringed birds but the problem with observing them is they all look the same whether they are resident or come on long journeys from far flung places like Iceland or Russia. There is ample food available for the birds in the ponds at Rainton Meadows, the fishing ponds in Fence Houses, large rivers like the River Wear, fast flowing streams like Lumley Park Burn and woodlands. Throughout the area on open farmland, housing developments, isolated farms, hamlets, villages and larger towns birds will find food from insects on farmland to bird feeders in private gardens. Some birds are easily seen and will live happily with humans such as robins. Other birds that will fly away from humans such as woodpeckers that can only to be heard by the sound they make or their birdsong. While nocturnal birds like owls that are rarely seen as they hunt at night and are rarely seen in daylight.

Birds and wildlife are under threat due to the damage man has done to our planet since the beginning of the Industrial Revolution over a period of 200 years. Climate change impacts on the Lumley area. Caterpillars appear earlier due to climate change which may mean a vital food source is less likely to be available to birds such as blue tits and robins who seek food for their young. Hedgehogs will find it harder to find food as dry, hard soil in summer make it difficult to find worms. Fires are more likely in woodlands if we have warmer and drier summers. The Woodland Trust warns us about the threats facing us when it says global warming affects all of us. But all is not lost. Not yet. We can all take action to make a difference.

 I have recorded my sightings of the birds that live and sometimes breed in our area during 2020 and 2021.The images are my best pictures from local, national and international locations where I observed birds. All photographs were taken by Robert Bishop. Most of the photographs were taken in the area around Great Lumley.

Rainton Meadows

Chester-le-Street Riverside.

Lamb Bridge Lumley Park Woods.

Hags Bridge Lumley Park Woods.

Chester-le-Street Riverside Park.

Lumley Park Burn Beacon Hill.

Lumley Park Burn between Brecon Hill and the Floaters Mill.

Old Waggonway to south of Great Lumley Village.

The Mute Swan (Cygnus olor) is our heaviest resident bird in our area and they are a common site in large numbers. They are found in Lumley Park Burn, River Wear, Rainton Meadows, Joe's Pond and sometimes on farmland. I have seen them nesting on the edge of Lumley Park Burn and on the ponds at Rainton Meadows. Their natural food is water plants, snails and insects, but they are quite happy to feed off humans in the Riverside Park. You have to aware that will get aggressive during their breeding season if their cygnets are disturbed. A mute swan was very aggressive towards a cormorant that was bothering the mute swan family as it was too close to the newly born cygnets. There is a large population of swans on the River Wear at Chester-le-Street with over 90 swans been found on the river in the winter months. In the winter up to 75,000 birds can fly into Britain from colder regions of Europe especially in colder winters, but the mute swans in our area are seen throughout the year in the same location. It always amazes me at how they can take off as they are such large and heavy birds. The River Wear acts like a runway for the swans as they use their powerful wings to take off and land on the long straight section of the river by the Riverside Park and its junction with the Cong Burn. The location to watch the swans throughout the year is on Joe's Pond and on the pond by the Rainton Meadows Visitors Centre where over 20 swans live amongst the Reed Beds Here you can watch them nest and bring up their families without causing them any interference or upset.

Mute Swan (Cygnus olor) Chester-le-Street Riverside photograph.

I have only once observed a Whooper Swan (Cygnus Cygnus) in the area at Rainton Meadows in April 2021 on an island in the middle of the ponds. They differ from mute swans as they are much bigger birds with yellow and black bills instead of the mute swans' orange coloured bill. They migrate to Britain from Iceland to feed on grain, grass and aquatic plants. Over 10,000 birds can migrate to Britain but few breed here and they are on the amber list of concern on RSPB classification who are concerned about the Whooper Swan. I have seen them in the lake in the centre of Reykjavik in Iceland in mid February and was amazed about the massive size of these swans that were literally skating around on the ice covered lake in the centre of the Icelandic capital city. These birds are rarely seen in our area, but attract a lot of bird watchers. Often these swans can be flying over the area as they fly at high altitudes of up to 8,200 metres that is nearly the height of Mount Everest to and from Iceland. In the Spring and Autumn, the best place to observe these birds is on the Ouse Washes in Cambridgeshire where up to 5000 Whoopers spend their winter months.

Whooper Swan (Cygnus Cygnus) Iceland photograph.

The Pink-footed Goose (Asner brachyrhynchus) is a bird I have only once seen in the middle of a group of Greylag Geese on Rainton Meadows. These birds are often seen in flocks flying over the North East as they migrate southwards during the winter feeding in places like the sugar beet fields of East Anglia. I was only aware of the bird as it was darker in colour and did not have the orange coloured beak of the Greylag Goose. It breeds in Iceland, Greenland and Spitsbergen in the Arctic and is often seen in large flocks flying overhead to and from spending their winters in Norfolk. It may have become mixed with the

Greylag Geese in the Arctic and have flown down to Britain with them. They feed on grain, grass, potatoes and cereals. They are often seen in this area when up to 19,000 migrating are seen flying over North East of England in the winter months and some would probably stop off on its migratory routes.

Pink-footed Goose (Asner brachyrhynchus) Rainton Meadows photograph.

The Greylag Goose (Anser Anser) is most commonly seen in and around the Rainton Meadows fields. The bird had pink legs with an orange bill and are pale grey in colour. They happily live alongside meadows with cattle and sheep. In the winter months their numbers are boosted by wintering birds when sometimes whole fields are full of hundreds of the birds. Over 80,000 birds arrive in November from Iceland to over winter and breed in Britain. The Greylag Goose is the largest and bulkiest of the Goose family. The fields around Rainton Meadows and the surrounding farmland that is under grass can have hundreds of Greylag Geese feeding on the grass. In December 2000 over 500 Greylags were recorded to be seen in the Rainton Meadows area. The birds feed on grain, roots and cereal leaves. They tend to fly in large flocks and often the Canada Geese intermixed with the Greylags.

Greylag Goose (Anser Anser) Rainton Meadow photograph.

The Canada Goose (Branta Canadensis) is seen in large numbers on the ponds at Rainton Meadows throughout the year with the numbers of birds rising up to 150 during the summer months. The Canada Goose has a black head and neck and large white throat patch. It is an introduced species is a from North America that spread to cover most of the UK. I witnessed some very aggressive behaviour when we walked near them at Lambton Ponds where there are flocks of up to 120 birds in the autumn months.

Canada Goose (Branta Canadensis) Rainton Meadows photograph.

The Shelduck (Tadorna tadorna) is a bird I first saw in Holland, but are rarely seen in the Lumley area. It is a large duck with a large red bill knob with a dark green head and neck with a chestnut coloured belly stripe. In the Lumley area I observed them in April when a pair of Shelducks floated on a small temporary pond near Houghton Gate and a few pairs were living on a pond in Rainton Meadows. The birds are not seen in this area throughout the year, but many Shelducks live and breed on the North Tees Marshes. The Shelduck have flown in from the North Sea coasts of Germany, Denmark and Holland. They nest in the nearby bushes or in hollows in the ground on the small islands of Rainton Meadows before flying off to locations within Britain or across the North Sea. The only way we would have knowledge of the bird's movement would be if they were ringed. The birds are bigger than mallards and smaller than most geese.

Shelduck (Tadorna tadorna) Rainton Meadows photograph.

The Mandarin Duck (Aix galericulata) was seen in Lumley Park Burn between Brecon Hill and the Floaters Arms in March 2021 on my walk down Lumley Park Burn. The mandarin duck is a bird I have never seen before this year. The mandarin duck is a resident bird that lives here all year. This beautiful duck was introduced from the Far East where it can still be found in China, Japan, Korea and parts of Russia. It has escaped or has been deliberately released from captivity in the UK and now breeds in the wild. Other birds that are non-native are the Ring-necked parakeets often found in places like London parks, Black Swans, Egyptian Geese, Muscovy duck and Red-legged Partridge. All of these birds which were imported from abroad and are now found in the wild having escaped or been released from captivity. It is a beautiful duck with the male mandarins have stunning plumage with orange cheeks, orange 'sails' on their back, and pale orange sides. The females are equally as beautiful without the stunning colours as they have grey heads, brown backs and white eye stripe.

Mandarin Duck (Aix galericulata) Lumley Park Burn photograph.

I first observed the Wigeon (Anas Penelope) waddling across the ice on Lake Tjornin in the centre of Reykjavik in a sub zero conditions in February 2019 with only one small corner of the lake clear of ice. The male wigeon is a dabbling duck and has a reddy brown or chestnut head with a strip of yellow on his forehead. The female was tawny brown in colour and a white belly and can be easily confused with the female mallard. The next time I was to see the Wigeon was on a pond on Rainton Meadows in June. Less than 500 pairs of wigeons reside in our country, but 440,000 birds migrate to our shores from breeding grounds in the autumn months from as far away as Siberia. It is likely these birds may have come from Iceland, Russia or Scandinavia. The birds are that live around lakes and look to feed on grasses, aquatic plants and roots. It is often described as a dabbling duck (a duck that feeds on the surface). It is often seen flying in tight formations and grouping on old gravel pits, wet grasslands and reservoirs, but only a few small groups are found on Rainton Meadows.

Wigeon (Anas Penelope) Iceland photograph

The Gadwall (Anas Strepera) is another dabbling duck seen on Ponds on Rainton Meadows or Joes Pond. There are only small numbers of these ducks that are smaller than mallards and are grey in colour with a black rear end. These birds winter here with up to thirty birds observed at Rainton Meadows and just over a thousand pairs breed in Britain. Over 25,000 Gadwalls migrate to our shores in winter. The female Gadwalls are easily confused with the female mallards. The birds that migrate from the far north of the European continent by flying at night and resting on ponds and lakes during the day. Many of our Gadwall will come from Iceland to escape their cold winters. They feed on vegetation around ponds. They will often follow other birds like coots that eat pond weed or other vegetation that they have brought to the surface. They will then steal this food from the angry coot.

Gadwall (Anas Strepera) Joes Pond Rainton Meadows photograph.

The Common Teal (Anas crecca) is a small dabbling duck seen on the ponds on Rainton Meadows with up to a hundred in the winter months, but in very small numbers in the summer months. The male ducks head is stunning with a chestnut coloured head with green eye patches, while the female is mottled brown. Only just over 4000 birds breed in Britain while over 200,000 migratory birds' winter on our shores after travelling from breeding grounds in the Baltic Sea area and Siberia in the North of Russia.

Common Teal (Anas crecca) Rainton Meadows pond photograph.

The Mallard (Anas platyrhynchos) is another dabbling duck seen throughout the Lumley area on streams, lakes and rivers. Britain has nearly 150,000 breeding pairs with over 700,000 ducks migrating to our shores from as far away as Russia. Over a hundred mallards can be seen throughout the year on Chester-le-Street Riverside and over 160 birds on Rainton Meadows in the autumn. Fewer birds seen in other months of the year. They have a varied diet with plants, insects, berries, acorns, shellfish and seeds. In the spring they often produce up to ten ducklings. The colours of the birds vary as they have breed with so many other ducks, but the male commonly has a green head and brown breast while the females are mainly brown with an orange beak. It is not uncommon to see white or black mallards or a variety of colours. Some birdwatchers call these cross bred mallards mucky ducks. They really don't like bread that is commonly feed to them as it is not good for their digestion. The mallards are an ancestor of the farmyard domesticated duck.

Mallard (Anas platyrhynchos) Chester-le-Street Riverside Park photograph.

The Garganey (Anas querquedula) is a rare surface feeding dabbling duck that I was lucky enough to see on Rainton Meadows ponds in August 2020. We are at the northern end of where they will migrate to in the British Isles. The duck winters are spent in Africa's sub-Sahara regions and it is rarely seen in our area. The female I observed looked very similar to the female mallard or teal. They normal are only found in the south of England and are our only summer migratory duck and are nicknamed a cricket teal or summer teal.

Garganey (Anas querquedula) Christopher Cadbury Reserve, Upton Warren, Worcestershire photograph.

The Northern Shoveler (Spatula clypeater or Anas clypeata) is a dabbling duck that is a surface feeder that are seen on Rainton Ponds all year round. They feed on crustaceans that they filter with their huge bills. The bird has a green head, a yellow eye and orange brown breast. The females are mottled brown. In Britain we have less than a thousand breeding pairs and they do breed on the ponds at Rainton Meadows. There are over 18,000 birds over wintering in Britain and then they migrate to continental Europe.

Northern Shoveler (Spatula clypeater or Anas clypeata) Rainton Meadows ponds photograph.

The Common Pochard (Arthya farina) is a diving duck that has a reddish brown head with a pale grey body and black breast. They are rarely seen on Rainton Meadows with only a couple of pairs of birds. On Rainton Meadows the Common Pochard has a pond that provide it with its diet of small fish, snails, seeds and insects. Less than 700 pairs breed in Britain but 38,000 birds winter here from the colder continental Northern and Eastern Europe breeding grounds.

Common Pochard (Arthya farina) Rainton Meadows photograph.

The Tufted Duck (Aythya filigula) is a common diving duck on Joes Pond, Rainton Meadows and the River Wear. It is a small black and white duck with a yellow eye. There are less than 20,000 pairs in Britain with over 100,000 birds coming from Iceland and Northern Europe over the winter months. There is a resident population on the River Wear by the Riverside Park. I seem to see them on every visit, but data says they disappear between August and October. Their hairdo is fantastic with a long tuft at the back of its head. They dive to find their food that consists of aquatic insects, waterweed and seeds. The female is a chocolate brown colour and they have eight to ten young ducklings. They are great to observe as they duck and dive and bob up and down. These ducks are regularly seen in large numbers on Joe's Pond and on other ponds around Rainton Meadows with a number of breeding pairs.

Tufted Duck (Aythya filigula) Chester-le-Street Riverside Park photograph.

The Goosander (Mergus Merganser) is a bird that is often seen diving on Lumley Park Burn and the River Wear. The male has a green head while the female has a red brown head. They had a long serrated bills and saw like teeth that are ideal for fishing and gripping fish. They belong to a group of ducks called sawbills whose slender bills are lined with backward pointed teeth that are ideal for gripping slippery and wriggling fish. Fishermen do not like them as they have a diet of river trout and salmon. They were originally bred in Britain in 1871 and now have a population of nearly 4,000 pairs and several of these pairs are found on the River Wear. Over 12,000 more Goosanders arrive in Britain over the winter months from Scandinavia and the Baltic States. The young Goosander will often sit on their mothers back as they glide along the river. They often build nest in riverside trees on the water's edge.

Goosander (Mergus Merganser) River Wear Chester-le-Street.

The Grey Partridge (Perdix perdix) is a bird I have only ever seen twice in the area. Some have said this is birds' success or failure is an excellent countryside barometer showing the health of our natural environment. It is a medium sized bird with an orange face, grey brown back and a dark black brown horseshoe shape on patch on its belly. The first sighting was in the field edge backing onto the housing estate opposite the Dun Cow public house and the second was in the fields on the opposite side of the road to Castle Dene. The birds were perfectly camouflaged by the hedges and fields where it feeds on leaves, seeds, caterpillars, beetles, weevils, flies and seeds. This is a rare bird in serious decline nationally and is on the RSPB Red List of endangered birds due to the removal of its farmland and grassland habitats. However, encouraging data has shown an increase in the birds locally as it is found throughout County Durham and 18 Grey Partridge have been seen on Rainton Meadows during bird counts. The Grey Partridge spends most of its life on the ground in a small area and will run instead of flying if disturbed. This partridge lays between twelve and sixteen eggs and the young are able to run around and feed themselves immediately after birth. The steep decline in its numbers is due to the low chick survival rate due to the loss of its natural habitats and the increased use of pesticides. Between 1870 until 1930 there was a Grey Partridge population of around 2 million living on arable farmland and enclosed land. The use of pesticide and herbicide removed much of the bird's food supply as chickweed and black bindweed was killed off. The hedgerow removal meant it lost a protective habitat where it could hide and lay eggs. The birds had little breeding success because of their predators that included foxes, ferrets, weasels and crows. They were often killed in pheasant shoots. They are a native birds that would be unable to fly over long distances overseas.

Grey Partridge (Perdix perdix) near Castle Dene
photograph using a zoom lens at long distance.

Pheasant (Phasianus colchicus) are instantly recognisable in
the countryside with their dark green and red head and
golden brown chestnut body markings and the paler brown
coloured females. They are seen everywhere in the area and
they are seen daily in the Lumley Castle grounds, on
farmland next to Lumley Park House and on the golf
course. These locations have lots of their favoured foods
with insects, grain and seeds. They are a native bird as they

wouldn't be able to fly long distances overseas. They are a very successful bird with over 2.4 million breeding females. They are a game bird with many pheasant shoots. Some of the Pheasants are bred in captivity and released after eight weeks or as adults to increase the number of birds for the shooting seasons. I will always remember the warning on the first tee on Chester-le-Street Golf Course that read 'PHEASANTS Please note that there will be gamekeepers here on Thursday 23rd Jan (2018) to control the pheasants who hid the last time. Please proceed with care'. The birds are always present on the course where they breed with several chicks. I once hit a daisy cutter shoot along the ground that flew past a pheasant and it jumped to avoid the ball a couple of seconds later. At the end of the breeding season, they can moult and lose a lot of feathers and look ill but this is just a part of its annual cycle that included moulting.

Pheasant (Phasianus colchicus) near Lumley Castle photograph.

The Little Egret (Egretta garzetta) has been seen in recent summers on Rainton Meadows. There are only a small number to be seen but these elegant white birds with black legs and greenish yellow feet are slightly smaller than the Grey Heron. They feed in the ponds by stabbing fish, amphibians and aquatic insects with their slender rapier like black bills. They were observed in the winter months and into spring between December and April. They have only been seen in Britain since 1989 when the were first seen in Dorset having travelled across the channel from North and

Western France. In the summer of 2021, I saw the first Little Egret nesting on the ponds at Rainton Meadows. As these birds move northwards it may be another sign of global warming as birds move northwards with a warmer climate.

Little Egret (Egretta garzetta) Gran Canaria photograph.

The Grey Heron (Ardea cinerea) is bird that is very common on all water courses and ponds in the area. They stand very still over water before striking quickly at its prey. They stand by the weir by the Riverside Park, in the shallows of the Cong Burn and Lumley Park Burn, at the tops of trees near the meander below Lumley Riding Farm and on the edges of ponds in Rainton Meadows. On the golf course they are often found in the trees hunting for mice and voles. This change in their diet is very important in winter months if their main source of food is cut off when low temperatures freeze ponds, lakes and other water courses. They also have a diet of ducklings, fish and amphibians such as newts and frogs. There are over 10,000 breeding pairs with another 60,000 who winter in the United Kingdom.

Grey Heron (Ardea cinerea) Hardwick Hall Sedgefield photograph.

The Little Grebe (Tachybaptus ruficollis) sometimes known as a Dab Chick is a smallest diving bird seen in our country with small numbers that have a diet of small fish, insects and larvae. They were observed by Hags Bridge on Lumley Park Burn and on the ponds on Rainton Meadows. We have over 10,000 Little Grebe breeding in the United Kingdom with 16,000 visitors from abroad. They are on the red list and considered to be at risk. They are amazing as the carry their young on their backs after hatching for a protected ride.

Little Grebe (Tachybaptus ruficollis) Rainton Meadows photograph.

The Red Kite (Milvus milvus) is a reddish-brown bird of prey that is commonly seen over the Riverside Park at high altitudes with its angled wings and its tell-tale forked tale. It is a great success story as before 2004 these birds were a passing migrant as they had been hunted to extinction. They had been targeted by taxidermist and egg collectors.

They were shot or poisoned by gamekeepers who believed they were killing game birds and livestock which was untrue as they only feed on smaller mammals, carrion such as road kill and worms. In 2004 they were reintroduced as Red Kite were released in the Lower Derwent Valley in Northumberland. In 2020 there was a count of 85 Red Kites in the area. A satellite navigation tagged and ringed bird was thought to have been shot near Derwent Reservoir as its tag stopped working. I have observed these birds over Beamish Open Air Museum and Waskerley Moor in the North Pennines. They reintroduction programme has only shown slow growth in the Red Kite population, but nationally they have been more successful with over 4,550 pairs.

Red Kite (Milvus milvus) Menorca photograph.

The Sparrowhawk (Accipiter nisus) is commonly seen over the area, but I have only twice seen them sitting on fences in Chester-le-Street gardens watching for any birds up to the size of a thrush as its next meal. The female sparrowhawk is up to a third larger than a male and has the ability to catch larger birds up to the size of a pigeon with their razor sharp talons. They are small birds of prey with long talons, yellow legs and bright orangey eyes. They hunt in small spaces like gardens and dense woodlands. These birds will not migrate overseas and are seen throughout the United Kingdom and our local area. The Sparrowhawk after World War Two were at risk as they had dangerous levels of pesticides building up in their bodies due to eating birds who had high levels of pesticides in their bodies. The chemicals were passed from prey to predators and by the 1960's many Sparrowhawks died. Fortunately, these pesticides were banned and the numbers of Sparrowhawks have recovered throughout our area.

Sparrowhawk (Accipiter nisus) Chester-le-Street woodland photograph.

The Buzzard (Buteo Buteo) can be seen anywhere in our area as they soar high in the air on hot summers days on rising thermal air currents. They are most often seen on the bridge over the A1(M) near the Smiths Arms area and in Lumley Park Woods. They are probably seen near the motorway as road kill is a major part of its diet. They were at risk due to chemicals used on farms up until the 1960's. Gamekeepers would often shoot them as they often ate pheasant chicks that were released to later be killed in future pheasant shooting. They are seen throughout the United Kingdom with over 150,000 birds. They are birds that soar to high altitudes with a shallow 'V' shape and vary in colour from light to dark brown in colour. They will hunt for smaller birds, small mammals and road kill, but will eat earthworms and larger insects when there is a shortage of food. I have often seen them perched on fences on the edge of Lumley Park Woods. These are native birds found in most parts of Britain and do not migrate.

Buzzard (Buteo Buteo) West Midlands photograph.

The Kestrel (Falco Tinnunculus) is a small falcon seen throughout the Lumley area. I have seen them diving into bushes from trees in Lumley Park Woods, hovering over the River Wear, sitting on garden fences and hovering over the A1(M). I have watched it consuming a small mammal on a telegraph pole near Castle Dene and hovering over Rainton Meadows. There most common location is near road verges where they look for road kill and small mammals. They have been called the windhover that describes how they hover over prey or the less glamourous name the motorway hawk. They did decline in numbers as farming changed with fewer hedgerows that meant a reduction in the small mammals that make up large part of their diet. They will eat worms, insects and small birds and I once watch a kestrel in my back garden as it hunted a small blue tit that was terrified in my back garden. The most common place to see them is hovering over roads and fields or at rest on lampposts and wooden telephone posts.

Kestrel (Falco Tinnunculus) Lumley Park Woods photograph.

The Moorhen (Gallinula Chloropus) is a common bird on the River Wear and Joes Pond near Rainton Meadows with their red beaks and black plumage. They eat small fish, worms, snails, grass, seeds, fruit, seeds and water plants. Over 300,000 birds migrate here for the winter from Northern and eastern Europe while 540,000 birds live in the United Kingdom all year round. The birds that are resident will stay in the same ponds and rivers for most of their lives.

Moorhen (Gallinula Chloropus) Rainton Meadows photograph.

The Coot (Fulica atra) is a seen on the ponds in and around Rainton Meadows and on the River Wear with their distinctive black plumage and white beak. On its forehead it has a white shield which the reason why bald men are often called as bald as a coot. They eat insect larvae, snails, vegetation and seeds. We have over 60,000 resident pairs with over 190,000 migrating visitors from Northern and Eastern Europe.

Coot (Fulica atra) Rainton Meadows photograph

The Oystercatcher (Haematopus ostralegus) is a common bird on the Seaham Harbour beach but are a common seen on Chester-le-Street Golf Course, the River Wear and

Rainton Meadows. They have orange legs and red bill. When flying they have a black tail and white wing stripes. They are looking for worms inland but are cockle and muscle eaters by the sea where their nickname is a muscle cracker. There are over 100,000 bird's resident with over 400,000 winter visitors from Scandinavia, Russia and Estonia. Over the last fifty years many birds have moved inland. In the winter they form together in large flocks in a tight formation making a lot of noise calling out kleep kleep. I have seen them as far inland near Tunstall reservoir above Weardale near Wolsingham in a sewage works.

Oystercatcher (Haematopus ostralegus) Chester-le-Street Riverside Park photograph.

The Golden Plover (Pluvialis apricaria) was a bird I first observed on Waskerley Moor as they flew in large flocks over man made reservoirs in North Pennine Area of Natural Beauty. They are a beautiful bird in their speckled gold and black breeding plumage. They nest on open heather moors and grassland. They lived next to the reservoirs and feed amongst the heather on high moorland in the summer months, before moving to lowland pastures in the winter months. They were seen in the fields between Castle Dene and Lumley Thicks in October. In the autumn months they feed on these open fields that had been ploughed. They are looking for insects, beetles, leatherjackets, ants, earwigs, caterpillars, worms, moth larvae, spiders, snails, berries and seeds. Over 400,000 birds migrate to Britain mainly from Iceland and some from Northern Europe to join our resident population that numbers almost 120,000 birds.

Golden Plover (Pluvialis apricaria) Smiddy Shaw Reservoir
North Pennines Area of Outstanding Beauty photograph.

The Lapwing (Vanellus vanellus) were seen as solitary
birds in the fields near Rainton Gate and in large flocks
over Rainton Meadows. They are members of the plover
family and can often be seen with flocks of Golden Plovers
and are sometimes known as Green Plovers. The resident
population of up to 280,000 birds have a diet of insects and
worms and are joined in winter by 650,000 migratory birds
from eastern Europe and Russia. They have declined in
numbers due to the modern farming methods that have
destroyed their wetland and marshy habitats. They are often

called peewits due to there call. They nest on open muddy or grassland and will gang up in large groups if any predators try to steal eggs of attack young chicks in their nests. Close up they have a beautiful purple green sheen but in flight in their flocks they look black and white. There most distinctive feature is their long crests on the top of their heads.

Lapwing (Vanellus vanellus) Rainton Meadows photograph.

The Eurasian Curlew (Numenius arquata) is commonly seen in groups in the late summer months after they have bred on the Rainton Meadows ponds, Lambton Ponds, in the fields near Lumley Riding Farm and between Castle Dene and Great Lumley. Often at around late afternoon in the summer months I will see several groups of Curlews flying from the south east to north west over the Riverside Park in Chester-le-Street. I have seen them on the Pennine Moorlands near Smiddy Shaw reservoir in the heather in the summer months as ground breeding birds. There are over 130,00 native birds in the winter and there are over 140,000 migrating birds from Scandinavia and Russia. They are easily identified with their long legs and downcurved bill. They have a diet of scrimps, shellfish, worms and insect larvae of beetles, spiders and flies. The birds were observed in the fields near Houghton Gate in April so it is likely that they were breeding in the fields in this area. Curlew with its long downturned beak is a migratory bird with some birds coming to Britain from Scandinavia to our warmer winters while other birds go to France and Spain from Britain. They can live up to thirty years of age.

Eurasian Curlew (Numenius arquata) Rainton Meadows photograph.

The Redshank (Tringa tetanus) was seen in the ponds on Rainton Meadows in pairs or as solitary birds. In the muddy shores of the ponds at Rainton Meadows they hunt for crustaceans, insects, earthworms and molluscs with there bills probing into the mud. In Britain we have about 50,000 birds with over 130,000 migrating visitors with about half of them coming from Iceland and others from Scandinavia. It is distinctive with its fine medium size orange black bill and long red legs. I have observed groups of over 60 birds roosting on the pier at Seaham Harbour in December. They are sometimes called the warden of the marshes as they make loud piping calls and yelps if there is any danger around the area. This warns other birds to be aware of dangers or threats against birds in the area.

Redshank (Tringa tetanus) Rainton Meadows photograph.

The Snipe (Gallinago gallinago) is a bird with a long straight bill and a gold and black head and a pattern of black and gold bars. I have only observed the snipe once on the ponds of Rainton Meadows in October. These birds were probably moving from their summer moorland bogs and wetlands in upland areas like the North Pennines. The bird struggles for survival as modern farming methods drain bogs and marshland. The benefits for man have been at the cost to birds like the snipe whose numbers have decreased due to the destruction of the wetlands and bogs that was once their homes. Rainton Meadows and Chilton

Moor are the home to at least ten snipe as a result of these post industrial sites having ponds on the old coal mining area. They were so difficult to see them as they blended in with the gravel on the islands in the middle of the ponds where they would be looking for worms, insects, flies, beetles and ants. The 160,000 Snipes in our country are joined by the one million wintering birds from Iceland and Northern Europe.

Snipe (Gallinago gallinago) Rainton Meadows photograph.

The Common Tern (Sterna hirundo) is a migratory nicknamed the sea swallow was seen flying low over the River Wear and hovering before diving under water to feed. On Joes Pond a different bird sat on green sign saying NO FISHING in an island in the middle of the pond and on other ponds in Rainton Meadows. They were observed on the beach at Seaham dive bombing into the sea after swooping low and hovering over the waves. They will plunge into the water to a depth of up to 2 metres. Sometimes they fly along the surface with their bill just dipping into the water to locate fish in an action known as contact dipping. In fresh water habitats they are looking for minnows, roach and perch. The birds have a black head, a folked tail and an orange beak and legs. The 24,000 of these fish eating birds live on the coast and inland and nest on shingle beaches, gravel pits and reservoirs. It is not a good idea to go near nests as the tern will attack intruders. I always remember a visit to the Farne Islands where the terns dive bombed tourists on the paths near their nests. They will migrate in the August as far south as the coasts of west and south Africa and return in April.

Common Tern (Sterna hirundo) Chester-le-Street Riverside Park.

I thought all the white sea birds were called seagulls. Gulls are often spotted inland and sometimes even miles from any coastal area because they have easy access to food and shelter. Humans make a tons of waste that many gulls find as free food. Gulls are expert scavengers. There is not a single species called the seagull, but people all over the world refer to them as seagulls. They are correctly referred to as "gulls. "with many differing species. Gulls are most closely related to the terns. Most gulls belong to the large family named Laridae. The word Laridae is from the Greek word meaning "ravenous sea bird." The term "Seagull" can be misleading because many species of gulls live, feed, and nest inland. In the Lumley area I have see many different species of gull.

The Black-Headed Gull (Chroicocephalus ridibundus) is a common bird throughout the area with large groups living around the River Wear and Rainton Meadows. The heads are actually chocolate brown not black. They live on insects, fish, worms and carrion. There are around 280,000 resident birds and another two million or more who over winter in our country from places like Poland and Finland. These are smaller than most gulls and in summer the head is dark brown. In winter the head is mostly white, with dark smudges on the ears and above the eyes. The bill also develops a dark tip. The birds Latin name actually means laughing that comes from the birds call that sounds as though it laughs.

Black-Headed Gull (Chroicocephalus ridibundus) Hetton Lyons Country Park lakes photograph.

The Common Gull (Larus canus) is a much smaller and cuter version of a herring gull. They often congregate on grassy land, playing fields or commons in villages which is how they came to be known as Common Gulls. I have only seen them twice firstly at Smiddy Shaw Reservoir in the Northern Pennines and secondly a couple of gulls making a real racket on a chimney pot on the Rivers Estate in Great Lumley. The adults have pale grey upperparts, yellow-green legs, a dark eye and a thin yellow bill. To confuse people like me trying to identify them the legs and bill are duller in winter and the head is streaked grey. Britain has just under 100,000 resident Common Gulls with over 700,000 wintering birds on our shores. Their diet is a mixture of worms, carrion, fish, insects and rubbish.

Common Gull (Larus canus) Great Lumley chimney pot photograph.

The Lesser Black-backed Gull (Larus fuscus) are a similar size to a herring gull. Adults are recognised by their slate-grey upperparts with blacker wing-tips and yellow legs and bill. They were often sitting in the middle of the River Wear shingle banks when the river is not in flood near where the Cong Burn enters the river. This shingle bank can be seen when the river in drier conditions was probably at the point where there was once a ford across the river.

These gulls are only seen in pairs or small groups around the area between April and September. They are seen at Rainton Meadows and around the banks of the River Wear often near groups of Black Headed and Herring Gulls. In Britain there are over 220,000 birds that are breeding and a further 130,00 birds' winter here from Northern and Western Europe and Russia. In early the early 1950's less than 200 Lesser Black-backed Gulls wintered in Britain as they migrated to Spain or North Africa, but they began to stop this migration as they could find a banquet of food on landfill sites. They are scavengers and are often found near rubbish tips and carrion, but they have a diet of worms, insects and vegetation on our inland sites.

Lesser Black-backed Gull (Larus fuscus) Chester-le-Street Riverside Park.

Herring Gull (Larus argentatus) is a more aggressive and intelligent gull who raid litter bins and will steal unattended food from humans. Most people call the Herring Gull a sea gull that does not exist. These noisy gulls are seen throughout the area with large concentrations at Rainton Meadows (with up to 300 gulls in spring) and Chester-le-Street Riverside. They like the ponds at Rainton Meadows and reservoirs where they can roost at night. The Herring Gull is a large sized bird with pale grey upperparts and pink legs. In summer they have a white head that develops darker at other times during the year. There are over 280,000 birds that are native to Britain but this number swells dramatically to over 740,000 wintering birds from Iceland and other parts of Europe such as Scandinavia and Russia. These omnivorous birds love rubbish tips and rubbish left by humans that supplements their usual diet of small mammals, young birds, eggs, fruit, seeds and carrion. They moved inland to landfill sites that were needed because the Clean Air Act of 1956 stopped the burning of rubbish that once caused smog in the larger cities of Britain.

Herring Gull (Larus argentatus) Chester-le-Street Riverside Park photograph.

The Feral Pigeon/Rock Dove (Columba livia) is seen everywhere in the area with larger concentrations around houses, villages and town centres. They eat seeds, cereals and human food waste with over a million birds in Britain. They can come in all shades and sizes as they had interbred with other pigeons and doves. The Durham Bird Club recorded over 120 pigeons at the Cong Burn outflow. They are very closely related to the Rock Dove.

Feral Pigeon/Rock Dove (Columba livia) Great Lumley photograph.

The Woodpigeon (Columbia palumbus) was a constant companion in our garden and on our walks throughout the Lumley area. These birds amaze me as they are so big and don't seem to fly far and are happy to be close to humans. They have cooing call that seems to be everywhere in the garden, parks, countryside, towns and villages. Our own native Woodpigeons number between 2.5 to over 3 million birds and they don't move far from their place of birth. Millions more Woodpigeons fly in for the winter months from place like Scandinavia. They counted over 400 Woodpigeons at Rainton Meadows in February 2020.

They love to eat crops on farmland like peas, grain and shoots and often farmers see them as a serious agricultural pest and they are controlled by shooting them. They will happily eat berries, seeds, nuts, buds and shoots in gardens, hedgerows and parklands.

Woodpigeon (Columbia palumbus) Lumley Park Woods photograph.

The Collared Dove (Streptopelia decaocto) is a bird that lived and raised several broods on our satellite dish outside our bedroom window with that lovely gentle cooing call. This Dove has always been seen nesting on or near TV aerials. They are much smaller and elegant birds than the woodpigeons with their grey colour and distinctive black collar. They were so tame that we could walk up to them in our garden and they would not move or fly away. They were happy in the garden eating seed heads, buds and shoots. In the wild they will eat grain and can form large flocks in farmers fields. They had at least three sets of dove chicks each year on our satellite dish. They are a very successful birds with nearly two million breeding birds in the United Kingdom. These beautiful doves are seen almost everywhere in the Lumley area, but have only lived in Britain since the 1950's when they moved here from Europe. They originally lived in the Middle East and moved northwards through Germany then to Britain when they were first seen in Lincolnshire in 1952.

Collared Dove (Streptopelia decaocto) Lumley Park Woods photograph.

The only Tawny Owl (Strix Aluco) I have ever seen in the wild was a juvenile bird at the entrance to the drive of Lumley Castle. It was a very big bird due to its juvenile feathers as it sat still high in a tree as if it was waiting for its parents to return with food that could be insects, worms, fish, frogs, rodents or small birds. I later found out you need to be careful around young tawny owls as humans will be attacked by mature tawny owls if you threaten or go too near to young owls. There are about 100,000 owls in the United Kingdom and adult birds have been observed in Chester-le-Street Riverside Park. The main reason for not seeing owls is because they are nocturnal and during the daytime you are only likely to see them roosting in woodland among ivy, in a hollow in a tree or against a tree trunk. The Tawny Owl tends to stay and live in a small area that is its own territory.

Tawny Owl (Strix Aluco) Lumley Castle drive photograph.

The Kingfisher (Alcedo atthis) is a beautiful bird that I have seen flying quickly with the azure flash streaking away at high-speed low over the River Wear in the Riverside Park heading towards the motorway bridge and Lumley Park Burn. It is often perching in reeds near Joes Pond and on vegetation on a meander on the Wear opposite the sewage works. I only saw it hoover once on the pond behind Joes Pond before diving and emerging with a fish in its dagger like bill. It then darted away in a low arrow straight flight over and away from the pond. They have increased in number around the area as the rivers and burns have become cleaner as industrial pollution has decreased. Places like Rainton Meadows that was once a highly polluted colliery have been developed to attract birds and wildlife. The number of UK birds has been estimated between 7,000 and nearly 13,000 birds. The estimated numbers of birds differ as less kingfishers survive after severe winter weather while they increase in mild winters.

Kingfisher (Alcedo atthis) Joes pond Rainton Meadows photograph.

The Great Spotted Woodpecker (Dendrocopos major) is a woodpecker that can be heard more often than they can be seen. The male bird has a crimson crown and there are up to 280,000 birds in the United Kingdom. These woodpeckers are most likely to be seen at the top of trees where they are looking for seeds, nuts. spiders, larvae and wood boring insects. These birds can be heard hammering away in Lumley Park Wood but never be seen. These birds have been seen on the golf course on the edge of Lumley

Park Woods and on bird nuts in our garden. In the wild I have only seen them in woodland in the Rainton Meadows site where young birds were been fed by there parents in a round hole in a tree trunk. These resident birds do not migrate and will live their lives in the area around where they were born.

Great Spotted Woodpecker (Dendrocopos major) Rainton Meadows photograph.

I find the Magpie (Pica pica) to be a stunning bird to observe with beautiful black and white colours, but on closer inspection it has a blueish purple iridescent sheen and a green gloss to the tail. The magpie is seen everywhere in the local area. A lot of people don't like these predators and scavengers. They are omnivores of the crow family that take birds eggs and are often seen at the site of road kill. When I observed a young robin been killed by a magpie it was very annoying and upsetting, but this is all part of the food chain. These birds will sometimes be shot by gamekeepers in areas where they are trying to protect some species of bird's eggs. We have over 1.2 million of these birds that are often seen in groups or even flocks. At Rainton Meadows flocks of over 50 birds have been observed in the winter months.

Magpie (Pica pica) Great Lumley TV aerial photograph.

The Jay (Garrulus glandarius) is the most colourful crow with a small black moustache, a pinkish fawn body with black and electric blue wing patches. I have only seen these shy birds in the undergrowth of trees in Lumley Park Woods and in small groups flying over or near ponds in Rainton Meadows. The Jay tends to live within 50 km of where it was born. They love acorns and were credited with the spread of oak trees after the last Ice Age. They also have diet of insects, fruits, young birds, bird's eggs and small mammals. Like all birds they have lost a lot of their woodland habitats as man has built houses and cleared woodland for farming. The Jay population is stable with up to 340,000 birds in the United Kingdom. Many birds have moved into urban areas where they feel safer than in rural locations where they may be shot by gamekeepers and managers of shooting estates where the Jay takes the eggs of game birds.

Jay (Garrulus glandarius) Washington photograph.

The Jackdaw (Corvus monedula) was a bird that was often seen pairs in the Riverside Park and throughout the whole area in abundant numbers. The grey hood and pale eyes are its distinctive features of one of the smallest members of the crow family. They eat insects, grain, seed, fruit, berries, eggs and young birds. They are equally at home on rubbish tips and eating scraps off garden bird tables. They are common bird with over 2.8 million birds. Most birds are native and will spend their lives within a small area of where they are born, but there are some migrant birds from Europe. I have often seen them on chimney pots where they have a habit of dropping twigs down the chimney causing many problems for the householder when they light their fires.

Jackdaw (Corvus monedula) Chester-le-Street Riverside Park.

The Carrion Crow (Corvus corone) is seen in large numbers throughout the area. They are a large crow that once attacked me when I was taking a photograph of them in the Riverside Park. We have over a million birds in the United Kingdom with a diet of scraps, eggs, fruit, seeds, worms and insects.

Carrion Crow (Corvus corone) River Wear Chester-le-Street photograph.

The Goldcrest (Regulus Regulus) is a colourful bird that was observed in our garden on the bird bath and in Chester-le-Street graveyard. They have a black and yellow stripe on the heads and are our smallest bird only 9cm in size. They eat tiny spiders, insects and moth eggs. We have over

600,000 birds with migrants from Scandinavia, Poland and Russia that make flights overnight to winter in the United Kingdom from October to March. It is amazing that this bird weighing six grams can travel such a long distance. They make nests from moss, lichen and spiders webs. North Sea sailors have seen goldcrests resting on their boats during migrations. They struggle during cold winters as they can use up to a fifth of there body weight keeping warm overnight.

Goldcrest (Regulus Regulus) Chester-le-Street Riverside.

The Blue Tit (Cyanistes caeruleus) is a colourful bird seen everywhere in the area with a mixture of green, yellow, blue and white. It has a diet of nuts, seeds, insects and caterpillars. We have over 3,600,000 birds and over 15 million birds over winter in the United Kingdom. I love watching them hanging to branches upside down and clinging onto brick walls. When I was young these birds would often peck off the foil milk bottle tops to eat the cream off the top of the full fat milk. They will mischievously be seen in our garden pecking away at string that is holding up plants.

Blue Tit (Cyanistes caeruleus) Chester-le-Street Riverside photograph.

The Great Tit (Parus major) is common bird in our garden that nests in our garden nest box. I once watched a Great Tit and Blue Tit fighting in the garden over a nesting box. They seemed to both want to nest in the same box. The

Great Tit is our largest tit that is green, yellow and black in colour with white cheeks. They are a successful bird with over two and a half million birds that have a diet of nuts, seeds and insects. They are found in large numbers throughout the area where most birds do not move far from where they had been born.

Great Tit (Parus major) Lumley Park Woods photograph.

The Coal Tit (Periparus ater) was an occasional visitor to our garden, seen on the trees above Nags Bridge on Lumley Park Burn and, in the bird, feeding area of Rainton

Meadows. The other sighting was in the stone slabs making up the wall of the ha ha outside Lumley Castle where they were nesting in the spring months. The black cap on its head and white patch on the neck area helps to identify these birds that feed on nuts, seeds and insects. They often take food and store it so it can be eaten later. There are 680,000 United Kingdom birds. It is one of the smaller tits and can sometimes be confused with willow tits.

Coal Tit (Periparus ater) near Nags Bridge on Lumley Park Burn photograph.

The Willow Tit (Poecile montanus) are a larger tit than the blue tit with a large sooty black cap extending down to the back of the neck. It is a bird in decline and is very difficult to distinguish from the marsh tit. There are only 6,800 birds in the British Isles and its population has reduced by 94% between 1972 and 2020 because their habitats such as in an old pit heap and rotten woodland that have been disappearing. The only place I observed this bird was on the bird feeding section of Rainton Meadows where it has marshy ground and ponds that these tits prefer as their habitats. They have been observed in this area nesting in a dead elder tree. The Willow tit has a diet of berries, seeds and insects.

Willow Tit (Poecile montanus) Rainton Meadows photograph.

The Sand Martin (Riparia riparia) flying over the Riverside is always a sign that it is Spring. Over 200 birds will fly over the River Wear near the confluence with the Cong Burn from April until they fly away in September. The birds were seen as early as the second week of March over Rainton Meadows. These birds are the smallest of the swallow and martin family with over a 100,000 birds in the country in the summer months. They eat gnats and small flies as the fly on the wing over water and nest in tunnels on river banks. They fly back to Southern and Eastern Africa for the winter months.

Sand Martin (Riparia riparia) Chester-le-Street Riverside Park photograph.

The Swallow (Hirundo rustica) is a common bird that I observed over the Riverside Park when they arrive in Spring until they leave in Autumn. The earliest arrival has been observed over the area in late March and early April. In early September over a hundred birds have been observed over Rainton Meadows. I have often seen them in large groups on telephone wires in the fields near Houghton Gate. There are over 860,000 UK visitors over the summer months until they head south to South Africa for the winter months. It is hard for the swallows to survive the long journey when they are vulnerable in stormy weather. They depend on food supplies on route. If they do not find a food source on their journey south it makes starvation a cause of fatalities. They swoop down over the fields between Houghton Gate and Lumley Park farm as they disappear into barns and farm buildings. They catch insects in mid air and build nests from mud and straw in barns, farm out buildings and under the eaves of houses. They are easily identified with their long-forked tail and dark red forehead and throat.

Swallow (Hirundo rustica) Houghton Gate photograph.

House Martin (Delichon urbicum) were first observed over
Chester-le-Street Riverside in early April when twelve
birds were observed and by mid July there were over 150
birds flying over the Riverside and over a 100 over Rainton
Meadows. The birds left the area in early October to return
to there wintering grounds in Africa. No one knows where
they travel to in Africa as it is a total mystery. These birds
with blue black upper parts and white rumps can be seen
over the Wear Riverside Park at Chester-le-Street swooping

in flight to capture insects and aphids. They nest in the eaves of buildings after collecting mud from the edges of ponds, streams and rivers in the area. Over a million birds fly into the United Kingdom each year and often return to the same nest to breed, but ornithologists are very concerned as they have seen the house martin population fall by up to two thirds of its former numbers.

House Martin (Delichon urbicum) Droitwich Spa, Worcestershire photograph.

I love seeing the Long Tailed Tit (Aegithalos caudatus) arrive in the garden or in the woodlands of Rainton Meadows and Lumley Park Woods. You see one bird then they are followed by several more in a small flock. The tail that is longer than its body is its most distinctive feature. Someone once described them as tennis balls on a stick.

They feed on insects and fly excitably in the woodlands and hedgerows looking for insects, moths' eggs, caterpillars and seeds. There are over 680,000 of these birds in UK that fly with an undulating flight pattern. I always remember seeing photographs of them huddling together in groups on branches to keep warm on cold nights. In late August groups of seventy or more birds have been observed over Rainton Meadows.

Long Tailed Tit (Aegithalos caudatus) Chester-le-Street photograph.

The Chiffchaff (Phylloscopus collybita) is a bird that is a regular visitor to our garden and is seen in woodlands in the Lumley area. It is a migratory bird that tells us that spring (usually in April) is beginning when it arrives. In early autumn at the end of September it leaves our shores. Warblers are so difficult to identify and I find real difficulty in identifying the difference between a wood warbler, a willow warbler, a chiff chaff or any of a numerous group or types of warbler. Apparently, it is helpful to listen to there voices but I struggle to identify most birds' voices unless they are robins or blackbirds. It all comes down to dark legs and a long yellow eye strip that gives it away that the species is a chiffchaff. We get over 1.2 million visiting chiff chaffs who love to eat insects that are found in trees, but it is agile enough to catch insects in mid flight. Some birds stay in Britain over the winter months as our climate is warming due to climate change. These birds weigh between 6 to 10 grams but travel each winter to sub Saharan Africa.

Chiffchaff (Phylloscopus collybita) Chester-le-Street Riverside.

The Blackcap (Sylvia atricapilla) is a bird from the warbler family that I have seen in our garden, Chester-le-Street Riverside Park and in the woodland near Joes Pond in Rainton Meadows. Some birds will overwinter in the North East, but I have never observed a winter resident Blackcap in our area. These birds are much easier to identify as the male bird has a black cap while the female has chestnut cap. There song sounds like a flute and they are called Northern Nightingales due to this song. They will eat berries and insects and we have 1.2 million of these birds visiting our shores each year. These birds migrate to Britain in the summer from Germany and north east Europe. They eat insects like caterpillars and flies and unlike other warblers they will eat berries.

Blackcap (Sylvia atricapilla) Chester-le-Street Riverside Gardens.

The Whitethroat (Currucca curruca) is a bird that I always felt as though it was welcoming us to Rainton Meadows as it sat on the telephone wire and on top of some hawthorn bushes. Apparently, these birds are quick, secretive and will hide away in scrubland and hedges. The Durham Bird Club have observed up to eight individual birds at Rainton Meadows in April. When I first observed the bird, it made me think of Father Christmas with the white feathers under its chin. It is a very small warbler that is a summer visitor with up to 74,000 birds that eats insects in the spring and summer. They will eat berries to give it strength before its autumn migration. Most migratory birds head for Africa via the Straits of Gibraltar, but these small warblers travel around the Eastern Mediterranean on there journeys to and from Africa with some going as far south as South Africa.

Whitethroat (Currucca curruca) Rainton Meadows photograph.

The Nuthatch (Sitta europaea) is a bird that can be seen on the drive up to Lumley Castle. It is a bird that has a mask and is seen climbing up tree trunks, along the branches or on the ground underneath looking for acorns and seeds. It is colourful bird with blue, grey, white and chestnut plumage. It never travels far from where it hatches and gets its seeds, nuts, acorns, beechmast and hazelnuts from deciduous forests like Lumley Park woods. They will often hide their food and return to eat it at a later date. They look a bit like a small woodpecker, but are only 14cms long that is the size of a larger tit. We have over 220,000 of these birds that are native to the United Kingdom and do not migrate. There whole existence depends on trees where they will nest in holes in the trees.

Nuthatch (Sitta europaea) Lumley Castle Drive photograph.

The Treecreeper (Certhia familiaris) is a bird that is so difficult to see or photograph as it moves so quickly in Lumley Park Woods near Lumley Castle and in the small strip of woodland between The Durham County Cricket Ground and the River Wear. It is a real beauty to look at with it speckled brown back and white front with long downturned bill that is ideal for plucking out spiders, insects and seeds from their deciduous woodland habitat. There are up to 200,000 birds in the United Kingdom and they will often join flocks of other small birds and tits in the woodland. I observed it flying in and out of its nest that was in an extremely small crack in a dry stone wall. Many birds feed, live and breed on the same individual tree throughout their whole lifetime and live within a small area of woodland throughout there lives.

Treecreeper (Certhia familiaris) Lumley Park Woods photograph.

The Wren (Troglodytes Troglodytes) is a small bird that has a dumpy appearance with a narrow tail that seems to be at a vertical angle from its body. It can be seen almost anywhere in the area in and around Lumley. The wren tends to live and breed within a small area. It scuttles around in the undergrowth and then hides under garden troughs. In Lumley Park Burn it pecks around in the muddy banks and by the River Wear it hunts for food of insects and spiders on tree branches. It is a successful bird that is native to Britain with over 8.6 million birds, but its numbers will fall dramatically during long and cold winters. It weighs the same weight as a one pound coin with only a few birds like a Firecrest (20p), Goldcrest(20p) and long tailed tit (50p) weighing less. Its scientific name means 'cave dweller'. It is known that up to 60 birds will roost in a bird box at one time in the winter months to share body warmth.

Wren (Troglodytes Troglodytes) Riverside garden Chester-le-Street.

The Starling (Sturnus vulgaris) has beautiful colours especially in bright sunlight where there iridescent black, green and purple colours speckle like glitter. They are seen everywhere in the area with their sharp beaks that they peck away in the earth. They love fruit and insects such spiders, moths, earthworms and leatherjacks. They fly around in flocks in the evening and can form murmuration's. Most starlings stay in the United Kingdom in winter, but some birds will migrate from Scandinavia and Russia in Northern Europe over the winter months. There are 1.8 million birds but their population has declined dramatically by up to 80% since the 1980's, but the bird watching organisations have not found a cause for this drop in numbers.

Starling (Sturnus vulgaris) Chester-le-Street Riverside photograph.

The Dipper (Cinclus cinclus) is a bird that can be observed easily in our area with the bird seen flying very low over the fast flowing streams like the Cong Burn near its entrance to the River Wear and over long sections of Lumley Park Burn. When I first observed them, it was like watching aquatic blackbirds with a white brest, but they are from its own dipper family rather than the thrush family. It bobs up and down and dives under the water looking stonefly larvae, caddis larvae, freshwater scrimps and insect larvae. It has a population of up to 37,000 birds and is chocolate brown in colour. To help them see under water the dippers have a third transparent eyelid called a 'nictitating membrane' that acts like a goggle to see under water. These birds spend their whole lives in a small area of a stream and are often seen standing on rocks or in one case a red road cone in the middle of streams. In the local streams as these birds defend their own territories vigorously.

Dipper (Cinclus cinclus) Lumley Park Burn photograph.

The Blackbird (Turdus merula) is a bird of the thrush family that is seen throughout the area during all months of the year. It is a common garden visitor and will come to the back door to eat dried fruit and is always drinking from the bird bath. They love apples and they enjoy the rowan berries in our garden and on trees by the River Wear. They will always be seen pecking away at the ground to eat the insects, caterpillars and worms in the earth. We have over a million birds in the United Kingdom that live here all year round, but in winter another 10 to 15 million birds arrive to spend their winters in this country. The ringing of migratory birds has shown that they have come from southern Norway, Belgium, Holland, Denmark and Sweden. The beak colour of the male birds is yellow with a yellow eye ring and the females are brown with yellow brown beak.

Blackbird (Turdus merula) banks of the River Wear photograph.

The Song Thrush (Turdus philomelos) is a bird commonly seen in the garden especially in cold winter weather. On walks this singing bird was always on the track outside Lumley Park House. This thrush is smaller that the mistle thrush. By the riverside we once heard a gentle cracking sound in the bushes and it was a Song Thrush with a snail in its beak. It had flicked a snail's shell into a stone with a flick of its head till it smashed leaving the undefended snail as a meal for the Song Thrush. There are over 1.2 million birds that love to eat worms and fruit, but they are declining in number on farmland and in urban areas. There fall in number is linked to the changes in land management where woodlands and hedgerows have been removed and there is less pasture land due to farmers cultivating more land. To identify it you need to look for the upside down heart shapes on its breast. Some of the thrushes in our area migrate to milder climes in Ireland while some Scandinavian birds are seen here as they fly south for winter. Many Song Thrushes over winter in our gardens and urban areas that are warmer than the countryside.

Song Thrush (Turdus philomelos) Chester-le-Street
Riverside.

The Redwing (Turdus iliacus) is one of our smallest
thrushes identified with orange red patches on its flanks. It
is not a common bird in our area and I have only seen high
in the trees in Lumley Park Woods and grazing amongst
thrushes on the golf fairway next to the drive going up to
Lumley Castle. Very few pairs breed in the United
Kingdom, but over 8.5 million birds winter here. They love
eating seasonal berries, apples and hawthorns in the winter.

When moving they usually fly during the night. The Redwings spend their summers in Scandinavia and Iceland then fly to the United Kingdom in September before leaving our shores in the following April. The Durham Bird Club recorded over 1200 birds flying over Sedgeletch on 17th October.

Redwing (Turdus iliacus) Lumley Park Woods photograph.

The Mistle Thrush (Turdus viscivorus) is a larger and greyer thrush with heavier and darker chest spots. It was observed on Chester-le-Street Golf Course and the

Riverside Park. It a more aggressive thrush and is a plumper powerful bird that has a diet of berries, insects, slugs and worms. They will aggressively defend its territories where foods like berries such as holly, hawthorn and mistletoe are located. There are 170,000 bird's resident in the United Kingdom with a name that is translated to devourer of mistletoe.

Mistle Thrush (Turdus viscivorus) treetop woodland photograph.

The Robin (Erithacus rubecula) is everywhere in the Lumley area. It will come up to the house and eat dried fruit and will hop along in front of you on country walks moving from tree to tree. It will aggressively defend nest boxes and food sources in a garden. They sing night and day with some robins singing next to street lights as it thinks it is next to the sun. We have over 6.5 million birds that eat insects, fruits, seeds and worms. We do get migrant birds from Scandinavia and Russian. Some of our birds fly south to Spain and Portugal but most of our birds live within a 5 kilometre radius of where they were born.

Robin (Erithacus rubecula) Chester-le-Street Riverside photograph.

The Dunnock (Prunella modularis) is also known as a hedge sparrow and to the untrained eye looks like a sparrow, but it does not belong to the same family. The Dunnock comes from the Accentor family and there are 2.3 million birds in the United Kingdom. Some dunnocks do migrate from Scandinavia to overwinter on our shores. The Dunnocks name comes from the old English dun meaning brown and ock meaning small. The bird identification is therefore known in old English as little brown bird. It is seen in our garden, on hedges in Scorers Lane and throughout the areas on farmland. The best way to tell the difference between a dunnock and a sparrow is by the beak shape with the dunnock having pointy and thin bill while the House Sparrow has a much broader and more powerful beak. It is a ground, tree and hedge feeder that eats seeds, worms, spiders and insects. They are an extremely common bird and will live within a couple of kilometres of where they are born.

Dunnock (Prunella modularis) Chester-le-Street garden photograph.

The House Sparrow (Passer domesticus) is seen on housing developments and gardens in Great Lumley. The bird is in rapid decline with the population dropping by 71 per cent between 1977 and 2008. This decline is caused by the change in farming practices with less winter stubble taking away a major food source. Farmers have improved seed collection and storage that means another food source disappears. They feed on seeds, buds, grains and man's rubbish and there are still 5.3 million birds in the United Kingdom population. The House Sparrow does migrate from the north and east of Europe to over winter in the United Kingdom.

House Sparrow (Passer domesticus) Chester-le-Street garden photograph.

The only location I have seen the Tree Sparrow (Passer montanus) is at the bird boxes at the end of the building at the end Rainton Meadows Durham Wildlife Trust Headquarters building. They are smaller than the house sparrow with a distinctive black check spot. The tree sparrow is a bird that lives in the countryside on farmland, hedgerows and woodlands and is very rarely seen in an urban environment, They have rapidly declined in numbers from 1970 to 2008 and there now only 200,000 birds in the United Kingdom. They feed on weeds, seeds and insects and the good news is a recent survey has seen a slight increase in their numbers.

Tree Sparrow (Passer montanus) Rainton Meadows photograph.

The Grey Wagtail (Motacilla cinerea) is a bird that often bobs up and down in the Cong Burn and Lumley Park Burn from rock to rock. It has a yellow breast and slate grey upper parts with a longer tail than other wagtails. There are over 75,000 birds in the United Kingdom and they like fast

flowing streams as a place to inhabit where they look for
ants, midges, snails and tadpoles.

Grey Wagtail (Motacilla cinerea) Lumley Park Burn
photograph.

The Pied Wagtail (Motacilla alba) is a bird I have observed
in the garden, on farmland and on the edge of ponds on
Rainton Meadows. In Chester-le-Street Riverside Park
where there are over 200 birds, they can be seen hopping
from rock to rock in the River Wear. It is looking for

insects and seeds and we have over 900,000 birds in the United Kingdom.

Pied Wagtail (Motacilla alba) River Wear Chester-le-Street photograph.

The Greenfinch (Chloris Chloris) is an olive green coloured finch that I have observed in Chester-le-Street Riverside park and our garden. I remember seeing many more of these birds when I was younger, but they seem to have become rarer and rarer. This has been linked to the birds contracting trichomoniasis which is a parasite induced disease from bird feeders in gardens that are not cleaned. There are still over 3.4 million birds in the United Kingdom and we have winter visitors from Scandinavia and Northern Europe. These birds have started to increase in numbers again in recent years according to recent surveys.

Greenfinch (Chloris Chloris) Chester-le-Street Riverside photograph.

The Chaffinch (Frigilla coelebs) is a finch that is seen throughout the area in hedgerows, gardens, woodland and parks. They are seed, caterpillar and insect feeders that are abundant in the United Kingdom with over 6 million birds.

Chaffinch (Frigilla coelebs) Chester-le-Street Riverside photograph.

The Goldfinch (Carduelis carduelis) is a bird that is stunning with it red and white head and yellow wing patch. There long fine beaks are perfectly adapted to getting to seeds on plants like thistles that other birds are unable to reach. We have over 2.8 million birds and some of our birds will migrate sometimes as far south as Spain. They are found throughout the Lumley area in woodland, farmland, parks and gardens. They will often be seen flying around in flocks in open locations like Rainton Meadows in the spring months.

Goldfinch (Carduelis carduelis) Houghton Gate photograph.

The Bullfinch (Pyrrhula pyrrhula) is a bird with a bright red pink breast and white rump that is commonly seen in the garden and on visits to Rainton Meadows. There are over 190,000 birds in the United Kingdom where they have a food source of insects, seeds and buds. There are some migrants from Scandinavia in the winter to our areas, but most birds will live in the same area throughout their lives. They are known by some as bud finches as they eat the buds of plants. Fruit farmers dislike them as they eat the buds that create the blossom to produce apples, pears, etc.

Bullfinch (Pyrrhula pyrrhula) Chester-le-Street Riverside garden photograph.

The Yellowhammer (Emberiza citronella) is a bunting I have only seen in the fields to the south of Lumley Junior School in the fields and hedgerows near the allotments. They flew around in small flocks mixing with reed buntings as they fed on the stubble in the fields in March.

They are a beautiful bird with bright yellow heads. There are 700,000 birds in the United Kingdom, but the numbers of these birds have declined by up to 50% in recent years due to hedgerow removal and a decrease in winter stubble on farmland. The yellowhammer usually lives within the same locality throughout there lives. Great Lumley is an area where there have been many birds observed with 60 or more birds been observed in the area which is probably due to several fields having been not vegetated and left with stubble on the land. Unfortunately, in 2022 there are plans to build on the land where I observed them which means another of there habitats has been lost.

Yellowhammer (Emberiza citronella)

The Reed Bunting (Emberiza schoeniclus) was seen on the fields of stubble south of Great Lumley village near Cocken Lane in March with the yellowhammers as both belong to the bunting family. In Rainton Meadows they are commonly seen in the reed beds and hedgerows. They eat seeds and insects and the male is easily identified with there black head. There are up to 250,000 birds in the United Kingdom and most birds live within a small locality over the course of there lives.

Reed Bunting (Emberiza schoeniclus) Rainton Meadows photograph.

The Linnet (Carduelis Cannabina) is a bird that I have observed on Rainton Meadows and on the coast at Seaham Harbour. It is a beautiful looking finch with a crimson forehead and breast. Its numbers have fallen dramatically by over a half in the last fifty years with over 430,000 birds remaining. It is a flower, bud, larvae, snail, insect and seed feeder that has suffered as its farmland habitat of stubble has changed with the intensification of agriculture.

Linnet (Carduelis Cannabina) Rainton Meadows photograph.

Bibliography

The Wildlife Trusts.

Royal Society for the Protection of Birds.

British Waterfowl Association.

The Woodland Trust.

Game and Wildlife Conservation Trust.

Durham Bird Club.

Printed in Great Britain
by Amazon

31718665R00069